T0147426

The New Universe

The New Universe

An Epoch Journey into the Sun

Kamakaokalani Lightness, MS

iUniverse, Inc.
Bloomington

The New Universe
An Epoch Journey into the Sun

iUniverse books may be ordered through booksellers or by contacting:

iUniverse
1663 Liberty Drive
Bloomington, IN 47403
www.iuniverse.com
1-800-Authors (1-800-288-4677)

ISBN: 978-1-4759-3015-3 (sc)
ISBN: 978-1-4759-3014-6 (hc)
ISBN: 978-1-4759-3013-9 (ebk)

Library of Congress Control Number: 2012910028

Printed in the United States of America

iUniverse rev. date: 06/20/2012

OUTLINE

ABOUT THE AUTHOR

Kamakaokalani Lightness M.S. is a graduate of Monmouth University, NJ. Her life's path brought her to Asia, Africa, North America and Polynesia. In 1975, her travels brought her to Honolulu, Hawaii. After her move in 1976, Kamakaokalani met a Hawaiian Kahuna, Morrnah Simeona.

During her studies with Morrnah, Kamakaokalani became acquainted with Ho'oponopono, the Hawaiian method of problem solving. Morrnah, in 1980, founded The Foundation of I, Inc. Freedom of the Cosmos. Kamakaokalani was the first instructor through Morrnah and taught classes in

Honolulu. Ihaleakala Hewlen began taking classes with Morrnah and Kamakaokalani during that time.

Morrnah and Kamakaokalani travelled extensively throughout the U.S. and Canada during 1980-1986. Kamakaokalani began teaching Self Identity Through Ho'oponopono classes in California and Colorado and was authorized at the time to coordinate classes in the U.S. and worldwide. Kamakaokalani began writing while living in Los Angeles and completed a screenplay, "Ascent to Infinity" in 1998. She completed a novel, "'Planet of the Crystals" in 2007. In 1998, while employed in Tinton Falls, NJ at a public school, she developed and implemented a Kindness Awareness Program for elementary school children. Through that program, a series of Children's Stories emerged. In 2009-10. She revised, "Planet of the Crystals" into" The New Universe".

Kamakaokalani recently retired from public school teaching and writes full-time at her residence in New Jersey, over looking the Atlantic Ocean.

I AM THE I

ACKNOWLEDGEMENTS

KA I

MORRNAH NALAMAKU SIMEONA-FOUNDER
THE FOUNDATION OF I, INC.FREEDOM OF THE COSMOS

THE FOUNDATION OF I, INC.FREEDOM OF THE COSMOS

IZILLC

THE LADY OF FREEDOM-AUMAKUA OF THE COSMOS

PLEIADES, INC.

INTRODUCTION

The New Universe encompasses the New Millennium from approximately 2000 to 2010, 2020's and into 2100 and beyond. The changes that are occuring at this time have been prepared aeons of time ago. All great teachers and sages have been aware of this. Many great souls have incarnated to participate in this momentous event

The New Universe is a series of books on Creation and the proper use of one's energy in creating a new life, HEAVEN ON EARTH.

HEAVEN is an energy field, a flow of multi-faceted dimensions which exists in the Pleiadian Star System. Earth was a part of that Star System, however, when time was created everything changed. Now, Earth and all that it entails is returning home to, "The Source".

Jesus or Joshua of Israel was from the Pleiadian Star System and appeared as Adam(Atom), Noah, Moses, Abraham Lincoln and others. He came to bring us home. He was one of those who incarnated time and time again to bring FREEDOM.

In the energy of FREEDOM exists the totality of ONENESS OF BE-ING with ONESELF and THE SOURCE of all life and existence. An earthly life then is an existence of pure bliss, or we might say, HEAVEN ON EARTH.

THE NEW UNIVERSE is an introduction, a mere fraction of topics which will be fully explored in the chronology.

Each page is complete. Each page serves a Divine Purpose as to hold in the highest regard, the spiritual ascent of those readers. Be joyous, be AS ONE, dear readers and create your own, HEAVEN ON EARTH.

HEARTSONG

THE HEART OF THE UNIVERSE IS PLANET EARTH. EVERYONE ON THE PLANET IS HEALING THEIR HEART. ONCE THAT OCCURS, THE SOUND EMANATING FROM THIS PLANE WILL BE HEART SONG. HEART SONG CREATES LIGHT. WITH THE EXPANSE OF LIGHT, MORE UNIVERSES ARE CREATED. THE DAY IS BECOMING LONGER AND SO EVENTUALLY THERE WILL BE NO NIGHT. WE WILL ALL BE LIGHT AND OUR FACES WILL BE LIKE SUNS AND OUR ADORNMENT WILL BE AS A RAINBOW. THE HEART SONG OF THE PLANET IS TO SET THE UNIVERSE FREE. UNI-VERSE IS ONE SONG, AND THAT IS THE SONG OF FREEDOM.

CHAPTER ONE

THE BEGINNING

What was created in the beginning was pure light This light was and is still in existence. It was the breath of life. Pure energy and vitality. It had no sound, it was like a sunrise on Mt Haleakala Quiet, noiseless, yet the most powerful vibration felt and experienced by ALL. Now, the ALL had been created. This was the very essence of life. When the light first emerged from Universal Mind, the ALL took it in. Then the ALL began to move into the ID. The ID being idea of Mind. The ID is movement of mind. Then the I came into BE-ING. The I represented form.

Before that time, there was no form. Everything just was. The I, the ID, the ALL are forms of life and Universal Mind. The Light, the Idea, the form being God itself. All of life came from Universal Mind itself. The mind is represented by The Original Sun of Suns. The Original Sun of Suns is the hottest core there is. Without this Spiritual Energy all of life would cease. All of life would cease. The I, the light, the ID, Idea, the ALL are the triune of Mind, and comprises the original atom of creation, LOVE.

Because we were in a perfect state of BEING, we needed NO-THING.

The I, the ID, the ALL is the undefinable atom of creation. This is LOVE.

God created LOVE to express itself in form and then function.

We are God's expression of itself. To consider us any less, or consider anyone else less is to diminish yourself and others. It is an insult to God and the Godhead itself.

Lady of Freedom

Chapter 1-THE EARTH

The New Universe is housed in the Central Sun. It is before the Sacred Rainbow of Creation and the One most High who overseas its creation. From the start, or the beginning it existed in the heart and mind of God.

GOD WAS, IS AND ALWAYS BEING GOD.

The Divine forces of Light, which permeate every atom of creation, are always being Light, always and forevermore. Within the LIGHT is all music of creation. It is within and without. Always in the Allness. The Allness is forever. It is eternity itself. Eternity is housed in the Heart and Mind of God. Within and without the Cosmos of Creation.

Now what is Creation? Pure Thought. When we have pure thought, we as spiritual beings are in a state of creation. A state of pure flux, a rhythm of being. With the Rhythm of Being is soul. Each one is unique with a

Divine Purpose. No one can know the divine purpose of a soul, except the soul itself.

The soul itself is always being the soul, unless it moves out of itself then it is bombarded by all kinds of thoughts. So it is important for the soul to be the soul.

The soul is a divine spark of creation itself wholly unique unto itself. A perfect pattern of creation itself. When a soul understands this pattern and acts on it, it is enhanced. It is a welcome note of joy to itself and the Universe.

We are constantly in a time continuum, moving this way and that. Much like the waves on the ocean. Each of us creates a perfect wave in the cosmic sea and when we move together as a unit of ONE, the entire cosmic sea moves. You might say we move the cosmos. It is not outside of us, but totally within our sphere of action.

We are responsible for our thoughts all of them, creating the next and the next and the next moment. All divine movement of mind is creating, THE NEW UNIVERSE.

Now this New Universe is entirely new, that is why the great teachers and sages greet each day (LIGHT) with such joy, for it is entirely new. We will see as we move through this sphere of activity more and more light and less and less turmoil. For we will see that the old thought forms are fading away and into oblivion. Transmuted into PURE LIGHT. It shall be thus.

As we open one door after another each one seeks and finds another door and another door. The portals of creation are endless. ENDLESS. It comprises continuous growth for a soul, on its homeward path into the HEART AND MIND OF GOD.

We are always growing and are constantly being supported by beams of LIGHT.
We are like sunbeams of LIGHT dancing on the waves of LIGHT which emanate from the GODHEAD.

The GODHEAD is the great, great, great Central Sun of creation itself. The brilliancy of this LIGHT is hard to describe, as it is so very pure. It is like fine exquisite crystal, a diamond beyond description. With this light is housed myriads of colors, which form a central vortex of light. Within this vortex is the very Breath of God. The ORIGINAL SOUND OF CREATION itself.

The Breath of God is the HA. This is within God, and within us too. As we breathe all of creation breathes.

7

Important to do the Ha frequently for it is the life-giving force of the Rhythm of Creation.

Water is abundant in the Universe. There are planets composed entirely of water. This water is composed of celestial bodies. These celestial bodies have a Divine Purpose for their own existence also.

Within these water planets are embryonic cells of creation, housing creation itself. To destroy any life form is an offense against creation itself. Abortion as it exists on Earth is a great misuse of the laws of the Universe and God. Those who support these thought forms are destroying life itself and will be held responsible for these actions. Totally and completely responsible. All of life is sacred and a gift of God.

In this New Universe are thoughts of love. For love itself holds the New Universe together. As love is holding this planet together, especially the continents at this time.

The continents are being moved as the planet is spinning more rapidly on its homeward path. We, on Planet Earth are experiencing high winds at times. This is due to the continents moving.

THE SUNS

Each Planet has many suns. Each Sun is a LIGHT unto itself. Each Planet is sacred and has a Divine Purpose. All work in conjunction with "THE SOURCE".

THE SOURCE AND I ARE ONE.

We are the SOURCE and THE SOURCE IS I. When we say, I AM, it is acknowledging THE SOURCE-GOD. We are acknowledging God, by saying I AM.

Some souls hear the singing of the Planets, or song of the Planets Some souls hear the song of the creatures upon and below the earth. These are both the inner and outer song.

The inner song is SOUL SONG. This is within the Breath. Within the breath is the sound of creation.

We are constantly creating with our Breath. Listen. Listen. Listen to the sound of your inner ear. What sound are you hearing from your own breath?

All creatures great and small have a unique rhythm of creation.

THE CENTRAL SUN

The great, great, great CENTRAL SUN is above ALL. Within the ALLNESS is life itself.

This forcefield of energy changes constantly as it is within the COSMOS of CREATION itself.

It is as a Giant Womb of God's energy. Within this Womb houses all of the energy of MATTER itself. We are, when we incarnate to a plane, planet, assume a form of energy of MATTER. A form of materiality that is aligned with our purpose and destiny for that particular incarnation. Everyone and everything has a Divine Purpose. For anyone to judge another, is saying I don't know whom I AM.

Remember, we are heaven sent. When we accept our DIVINITY, we accept our PURPOSE. Yes, we may be guided, but accept your heart's calling. For within and without, we are becoming all we were created to be.

CIRCA 2020's

Everyone is dis-ease free, in perfect health and wealth. All are guided by their high selves, aumakuas in fullfilling their Divine purpose and Destiny this lifetime. All souls incarnating are purposely created with spiritual guidance from The Source.

There are no unwanted children. There is no abortion. There are no hospitals, as everyone has the knowledge of healing themselves. Children are born in birthing centers, totally in an aura of LOVE. Products are reviewed by towns and regional committees to determine what is most appropriate for all concerned. There is no waste. All products are recycled. Everyone contributes to the maintenance of their homes and community. There is no welfare, it doesn't exist. There are no locks on any doors, as everyone is safe in their community. Crime does not exist. Everyone, including children vote for elected leaders who support themselves financially. All are represented. Leaders serve part-time only. All nations signed the GREAT ACCORD OF PEACE and outlawed war and instruments of war. Poverty and lack do not exist. It is a world of Peace and eternal rest. Stress does not exist. We will all have come home at last.

This vision of PEACE ON EARTH exists right now in the Heart and Mind of God. Once we know our I dentity as a child of God, then we really know, who we are.

ENERGY GRIDS-THE NEW ENERGY SYSTEM

High-energy grids powered by solar energy are built into various sectors. Moving vehicles are programmed to encapture the energy waves, similar to microwave frequencies and wireless technology. This is completely fossil fuel free. Current vehicles can be adapted and sensors on roadways will assist in these computer programs. Energy strips are placed on walls and floors in current dwellings of homeowners. These strips emit high frequency solar rays to heat, light and cool the homes.

Town centers maintain the energy grid systems that provide free energy to moving vehicles and homes. Aircraft are spacious and light and are powered by crystal solar cells.

Energy Domes are placed over entire sections of land providing tranquil weather. Dome Homes are built maintenance free. Water and trees are abundant and gardens surround the home. Fruits from the gardens and trees are nourishing and available. These fruits provide whole foods, a vegan lifestyle is easy to maintain.

Homes are minimal in cost, $1000 per home, and last for hundreds of years.

The monolithic dome homes are a step in the right direction.

All walking, biking and vehicle paths are lighted with solar sun cells, providing free and easy access to all individuals. With the ascendency of souls on Planet Earth, a more gentle, kinder and more loving energy will permeate the atmosphere. Bringing it to a more pristine state.

POLAR ENERGY

All of the energy of the Sun, our Sun comes out of the Polar Regions. The North Pole creates the entire weather system for our planet.

The Polar System is the backbone of the earth, which connects the North and South Poles and acts as a giant thermometer.

It constantly adjusts the meridians and crystal grid system, which comprise planet Earth.

Earthquakes are thought forms being released from the planet. Mother Earth needs the oil, to make adjustments in the tectonic plates. Oil is the blood of Mother Earth, needed to lubricate the crystal grid system for earth changes. The oil taken from Mother Earth must be done with great care.

No oil is to be taken from the Polar Regions, it could cause a collapse of the crystal grid system. If the crystal grid system ends Earth will disappear in shock waves.

For example, there is oil underneath the Continental Shelf on the Eastern Coast of the United States. If it is depleted the Shelf which has been slipping for quite some time, will collapse entirely.

With the proper use of ego and will we can create release all of these elements.

VOYAGE OF RE-DISCOVERY

EARTH is part of the Solar System and part of Galaxy 1 and the Milky Way. Our stellar systems are interconnected in ways that would baffle the human mind.

There are rings within rings within rings that create miniature star systems that are so intricate, no one knows about them. They have yet to be discovered by scientists.

Once we begin to truly understand the depths and breath of the human aura, only then can we begin to understand the cosmos. Remember, we create the cosmos, it is within us, not outside. Actually, nothing is outside of us.

The Ancient Ones, sages and teachers of the past were well aware of many areas of life, we are just now re-discovering.

You might say the Millennium Mind is on a Voyage of Re-Discovery of himself or herself.

CHAPTER TWO

NEW CREATIONS

ARGOS was the main center for production of the Pacific Crystals, it is near Tahiti. It still exists, although not as powerful as in the days of Lemuria and Atlantis.

One of the Sun's main responsibilities is to power the Earth and the Solar System. This is done through concentric solar rings. During the Solar flare, it is like a tune-up for the Sun and Earth. and the Crystals that it energizes. In turn, the Crystals send information back to the Sun.

The Sun works with all forms of life. Flowers, FLOW-ERS, and butterflies have genetic codes on their petals and wings. You may consider butterflies angelic spirits. The flowers co-create with the butterflies the genetic codes for a particular area. The use of pesticides disrupts all forms of life. It is deadly to creation. The chain of genetics is then broken.

War, of course is even more terminal to planetary life and evolvement. The main purpose of all Life is EVOLVEMENT. I will state that again, Life is about EVOLVEMENT.

Life is always in an upward spiral. Humankind has the most freedom to evolve. How an individual soul chooses to use or abuse that energy is paramount not only to that soul, but to all universal life.

Patterns of creation are UNIVERSAL

UNIVERSAL LAWS must be followed for ALL TO EVOLVE.

When the MAIN CRYSTAL was shattered by an inharmonious thought, aeons of time ago bits and pieces floated away becoming quadrants. The quadrants became like time capsules. Time was created, it did not exist previously. We all existed in a state of pure perfection. PURE LOVE.

God's love is eternal. NEVERENDING. It is the NEVERENDING STORY.

During the time of the great explosion universe after universe was created. Within these spheres of influence, life forms were created that now permeate the very ether of our existence.

All of these bodies are now changing into pure light. Pure light which is it's original essence of existence. Life as we know it was at a much higher level of existence.

Only thought, no sound was heard. We communicated telepathically. It was sufficient and thoughts were instantaneously manifested. There was no time gap.

Remember time did not exist for aeons. So, aging did not exist. We were pure thought in the heart and mind of God.

The God essence is contained in an original IDEA.

This IDEA originated with THE ORIGINAL SUN OF SUNS. The ORIGINAL BEING who created all life forms including ITSELF. This being was represented by ADAM OR ATOM. This great being of light incarnated this lifetime, however has returned home, and is waiting for the rest of Creation to return to THE SOURCE. After that, we will exist in a pure state of light and love, as we did in the beginning before the COSMIC EXPLOSION.

We are in the process of New Creations for this time period and place. The destiny of Planet Earth is to be an intergalactic solar system, which will propel THE NEW UNIVERSE into expanding LIGHT. This LIGHT is ETERNAL.

UNENDING. We as spiritual beings are creating our own eternity. That time is NOW.

Children are memories.

Some souls do not have to have children of their own. They have completed this learning task Others have chosen to be parents, and that is a unique responsibility, not to be considered lightly.

It is a SACRED TRUST. It is from the beginning of conception, when life begins.
LIFE BEGINS AT THE MOMENT OF CONCEPTION.

Couples, MALE AND FEMALE are to be in a PREPARED STATE OF CONSIOUSNESS.

The sharing of life energy is a Divine Act, to be done with reverence and respect for both souls involved. The child or soul coming through can be prepared before conception.

Remember each of us is a SUN.

Those forms that are cloned have no souls. They are devoid of Divine Energy.

Anything cloned is DEAD MATTER.

When we are in balance, spiritually, mentally and physically, pro-creation takes place easily. Artificial insemination is artificial.

The birthing and those attending the birth are very important. Both parents are in a state of receiving a very special gift from God. In some cultures, parenthood is the highest vocation. A couple may spend 5-7 years aligning themselves in a loving relationship before pro-creation occurs.

Each soul coming through is Divinely purposeful. CLARITY OF MIND IS A MUST.

In the beginning was the word. This was the sound and vibration of God. Lightning and Thunder are part of that Original Creation.

IT WAS AND IT IS.

Fireworks are memories of the ORIGINAL CREATION. Each planet is a Crystal Creation and creates a LIGHT FREQUENCY. The Light Frequency is within the SACRED RAINBOW OF CREATION.

All was and is of LOVE.

Before the Tower of Babel, we spoke only one language, the language of the heart. It is the sound of love. Love of self and others.

Planets are created to assist us in evolving as souls. Each one is important. Many planets and star systems that are part of The New Universe are also fulfilling their Divine Purpose.

Remember, there is no out there, it is all within us.

Mars was created to ground our energy, Venus is about home and hearth. Chocolate came from Venus, in addition to other fruits. Our physical ear formation usually indicates the most recent planet where we are from, before Earth time.

We are celestial beings playing in God's Universe. However, memories of the past have kept us stuck in stuff. Thought forms re-playing endlessly. We all can let go and ascend, it is up to that soul.

Souls are choosing parents, relatives and friends to assist them in evolving. Babies are meeting and having fantastic conversations with one another. Parents are surprised. However, there is that soul recognition. "Oh, they say, to one another, so you're here too".

PORTALS OF LIGHT

Throughout creation. portals exist. The portals represent passageways of time and dimension. The Polar Regions are major ones. The North Pole circumnavigates this current Universe, and is playing a major role in the Creation of the New Universe.

Perhaps those souls who have been guided to the North Pole are aware of this. Once a soul has this experience, the dimension of time changes for them.

Time is circular, not linear, as many believe.

You might compare it to a ball of light, which continually bounces through space. It has an up and down motion, entirely dependent on the thought forms created in the mind. We create time, by our existence.

There is no aging. Aging is a memory. Once we have released this memory, we will cease to "grow old". We will then grow, "more aware".

The Aurora Borealis is a passageway for souls to enter and exit the Planet. Many indigenous peoples were very aware of this fact.

There was a crystal dome over Stonehenge at one time. This created a symphony of Light and sound. In this energy was created an aurora borealis. This aurora allowed souls to enter and exit the planet, dimensions and universes. It acted like a time machine. Many souls who wandered there aimlessly were caught up in the energy (force field) and disappeared forever. One must be very grounded before going there, as the energy still exists to change one's biochemistry. There were 15 pillars that rang with sound, creating an opening into the heavens., at one time. Starships also landed at the site at certain equinoxes, to absorb these energies.

The core of this Planet Earth can create light everlasting. Complete daylight forever. We have only to adjust our minds to this fact.

Five Atlantean Temples of Light were over the Huber Woods area of Navesink in Monmouth County at one time. Three still exist today. Each housed a particular sound which kept the land intact. All worked in harmony with one another. They resonated with the other Temples of Light, which were located throughout the Eastern Seaboard of America, and included those above the Atlantic Ocean.

Beneath the Temples were underwater cities, which permeated many other areas including the Caribbean, and Florida. It was an enchanting and peaceful place of existence. Both Lemurian and Atlantean leaders worked together to preserve this way of life for thousands of years. Atlantean Kings and Queens lived in Eastern and Western Monmouth County, including the Highlands. They overlooked the Capitol of Atlantis, which is now New

York City. Their faces showed the light and love for all of life and creation. When their heart centers began to close, their faces became hardened, until these souls emitted no light at all. Then society began to crumble. Discord and disease emerged from this previous tranquil society. Eventually, fighting broke out among the Peacekeepers and so the land broke apart and sunk. All went below the sea.

Humankind is beginning to awaken from the sleep of the ages in preparation for the Great Events coming in 2012 and beyond. The New Universe has been prepared for those here now, centuries ago.

CHAPTER THREE

ASCENDENCY

Every place on the planet has within itself a Blueprint for perfection. All are moving quickly into the Light, as Earth begins its final ascent into the Heart and Mind of God.

Within each country is implanted a Crystal of Creation. This Crystal powers all of the other Crystals.

Egypt and the Sahara, (which was a fertile plane) is one of those places which has crystals still intact. This is one of the reasons Akhenaton established a new city of

Marrna. He came from a star system far from earth, but brought with him the knowledge of the Sun God, Aten.

Hieroglyphics is really a system of energy and sound. The hieroglyphics energized the land and the crystals. The Egyptian Pharaohs, both men and women were aware the land was sacred. In caring for the land and peoples all of life would flourish.

Slavery only came into existence when trust with God was broken. The sages and holy people were able to levitate not only themselves but the obelisks and other artifacts. Certain pyramids rejuvenated the auras of those who had that knowledge.

Actually, the healers of those early times were far more advanced then what we currently experience in the medical profession today.

Within the Sphinx was a main crystal and other secrets. This crystal powered the Third Eye of the Pharaoh. Only the Pharaoh was able to enter the secret chamber.

The Nile came into being, when the Pharaoh with the use of the crystal created a body of water. This then enabled the land to be fertile and abundant.

These power generators (crystals) provided all of the Light for the Cities of the Sahara. These cities were established as star portals for those from other planets to land and share their knowledge. They are now covered by tons of sand.

What is ascension? It means moving into a higher dimension and frequency.

Allowing oneself to let go of the old energy and move into the new, that is more purposeful for oneself and others. It is re-claiming our birthright, as a child of God, a soul on its journey into the New Universe. Thousands of souls are doing this, many in a very quiet way, without fanfare. Yet their energies are global in nature and vibration. Many organic products and companies are very aware of their responsibilities in this respect.

Earth is in a continuous upward spiral, coming out of the chaos and confusion of the past. This change is happening at every level both on the inner and outer planes of creation. We are all in for the ride of our lives.

When all of the aumakuas descend to this plane, there will be a golden light around the planet. It is GOLDEN DAYLIGHT. The GOLDEN DAY will be eternal bliss.

Those souls who have been steadfast in their spiritual resolve to be AT ONEMENT with all of life and creation will feel very much AT HOME.

Our sweet, sweet Earth will be the plane of sages and teachers, not through mankind's courses of self-awareness, but through their own evolvement and ascendancy. Ascendancy is from many lifetimes of learning both on this and the other side.

New souls are coming in, Many for first time on Earth and are bringing great joy and happiness with them. They are here as Rainbow Children of the New Universe. They have much to teach all of us.

Begin your day in humbleness and thankfulness. Acknowledge The Source, as you break bread for the Day. Do thank THE DAY for being.

In the creation of THE DAY, the energies that are involved, would boggle the human mind and even the fastest computers to date. All of those machines are at a very simple state as yet. Each DAY is created by Universal Mind for our greater growth and evolvement.

CHAPTER FOUR

COMPLETION

As the portals of the Earth open, GREAT COSMIC UNIVERSAL FORCES penetrate below the Earth. More and more LIGHT will emerge.

Global warming is Earth changing into a Brilliant Star.

In doing so, the Light expands and expands and the New Universe will make itself known, as the epitome of God's love for us.

The Planet will then have reached its completion as one of God's creations.

Every Planet has its destiny and Divine purpose. Those souls on other planets are aware of this and applaud those here now who are in their ONENESS. They are an example for us all.

The Planet must reach a certain vibration and frequency in order for many changes to happen. These great beings of Light who are coming, are so powerful, that their energies could cause a meltdown in our electrical grid systems if they were to suddenly appear.

So, the planet is being cleansed of all energies that are not in the love vibration.

When the moment arrives we will all know it.

We are the seeds of LOVE. To shine as loving beacons of LIGHT for all.

Now, you may ask, what is life like for an Aumakua. First, depending upon their blueprint, some will be observers. That involves great responsibility for self and others. Love and humbleness of mind are the keynote. For without these traits, egoism creeps in.

THE MIS-USE OF EGO CAUSES DIS-EASE, THE MIS-USE OF WILL CAUSE DEATH.

We are the creators or destroyers of our life force. OUR LIFE FORCE IS A GIFT FROM GOD.

The transformation of this plane will affect every area of modern life.

The educational system will experience much. Aware students will be teaching the teachers.

We will become taller and more elongated and move with the rhythm of the celestial forces. Our foods and dress will change.

Sun Centers will emerge. Montreal is an ancient Sun Center. All of Canada is a major portal of Light for the entire Universe and the Cosmos. Its proximity adjacent to the North Pole is crucial to the Light on the Planet.

As new crystals are imported into our sphere of influence, the meridian system of the Planet will flex. In this flexing the rhythm of life will change. We will all come to know that we have experienced many lifetimes in order to complete our earthly journeys.

Once the crystals that are housed under the North Pole become activated, the overseers, the Elohim will make themselves known, only to those that are to be aware of this. The Meridian system keeps us all intact. The Cosmic meridian system is complex and requires great discernment of mind.

We will come to feel the joy and peace that exists in the higher dimensions. It is only in our separateness from the Source that we experience unhappiness. Happiness and joy are our NATURAL STATE.

CHAPTER FIVE

AND IT IS DONE

Many places will emerge as Sun Centers. These MILLENNIUM CITIES will have prominence as land changes occur.

The United States is to nurture these future cities, it was one of the purposes in founding this country.

George Washington was quite a clairvoyant he and Ben Franklin had discussions on this very subject. All of the signers of the Declaration of Independence met again in

Philadelphia in 2000. Those and others have incarnated this lifetime.

Since interplanetary travel will play a major role during the Millennium, places with large free spaces will be important. The present day airports will be unable to function in this new role. Space Hubs will be set up to receive these interstellar travelers and their starships.

In the next 50 years our reliance on fossil fuels will diminish. This will not only clean the planet, but also eliminate smog. The smog is created by the pollution of mind. Ceaseless chattering of the intellectual mind. It is within the sub-conscious mind that is all knowing.

Those souls who have knowledge of themselves are here now and will be heard.

When the original star clusters broke apart, all knowledge of star charts were lost.

The star charts are the meridians to our home in The Sun of Suns. As we come into our ONENESS, we will create on the physical level the path homeward.

We age as our SUN CENTERS diminish and grow and evolve as our SUN CENTERS increase.

Love is the key to all evolvement. LOVE OF SELF FIRST AND OTHERS SECOND. Remember outside is only a reflection of inside. ALL IS WITHIN THE SELF. GET TO KNOW YOUR IDENTITY.

All planes of life exist at the same time.

There is no separation in Divine Mind.

Heaven and Earth exist at the same time. The veil between these two energy force fields is disappearing. The time is coming when we will see and experience those on the other side with ease.

As we come to know, we are heavenly beings having a human experience, our world will change. Some souls have been human too long and have forgotten who they are and why they are here. Our Identity as a child of God is paramount. It is not based on clan or family.

All of those are humankind's labels.

Our names are to be chosen with that in mind. Indigenous peoples and cultures choose a name very carefully. Sometimes a grandparent or elder will be aware. Our names are completely individual and cannot be passed on. The correct name is a blueprint for a soul's future. Wrong names disrupt our blueprint and our rhythm. Everything has energy.

The next time you crack open an egg, look carefully. Why do we say sunny side up?

Yolks are suns. We are literally and figuratively eating SUNLIGHT. We are beings of LIGHT, eating LIGHT, swimming in the LIGHT, bathing in the LIGHT etc.

Yet, we wander in the wilderness of mind creating darkness with our thoughts.

Forgiveness of self and others is the greatest healing energy on and off the Planet.

It is total surrender and letting go of all mis-use of ego and will. Unlimited love for self and others.

It's not about acquiring things outside of self, in order to change. It is about changing one's self first, then other things can follow. CHANGE IS AN INSIDE JOB.

By knowing who we are and our Divine Purpose and destiny, we can immerse ourselves in the task at hand.

Bringing ourselves into balance, spiritually, mentally, physically and materially with all of life and all of creation. It is in the ONENESS OF ALL OF LIFE AND ALL OF CREATION THAT WE FIND THE GREATEST FULFILLMENT AS A SOUL. Until that concept permeates our life, we will continue to be seekers.

The truth will set you free. The Truth is knowing who you are, and that is FREEDOM.

WE ARE ON A JOURNEY THROUGH THE STARS AND BEYOND.

WE ARE THE STUFF STARS ARE MADE OF.

WE ARE THE STARS.

WE ARE THE HEAVENS AND THE EARTH.

WE ARE.

WE ARE.

WE ARE.

AND IT IS DONE.

BIBLIOGRAPHY

Planet of the Crystals, Kamakaokalani Lightness-July, 2007

Unpublished-Library of Congress TXU 1-325-455.

THE PEACE OF I